is there an answer
anguished thoughts of a young man

by Scott E. Force

is there an answer
anguished thoughts of a young man

© 2020 by Scott E. Force

All rights reserved. Except as permitted under the United States Copyright Act, no part of this publication may be reproduced or distributed in any form or by any means, or stored in a database or retrieval system, without prior written permission of the publisher.

ISBN: 978-1-952956-00-3

Dedications

To my parents,
who never knew
the demons of my teen angst,
but were always there.

To the US Army,
where I found my answers.

is there an answer
anguished thoughts of a young man

by Scott E. Force

Contents

the question	1
for you	2
mr. fix it	2
on the side	3
ignore	4
as it should be	4
losers	5
did i stutter	5
yesterday needs tomorrow	6
you know	7
teasing	8
the candle is out	9
hold	9
the big world	10
how may i help you	11
hey?	12
there you go	13
yon	13
clear	14

waiting	15
a void	16
what i'd give	16
imbalance	17
the end	18
i've got them	19
serious	20
in the music	21
dial tone	21
a long day	22
in the lies	24
the new game	25
in the dark	25
it's not about winning	25
not much	26
in your hat	26
traveled road	27
is there an answer	28
summer's gone	30

is there an answer by Scott E. Force

the question

Just once won't you
give me hope?

You leave me,
I leave you for dead,
for me.

There is a question
you won't answer
for me.
What about me?

You avoid the issue
time and time again.
One of these times
your luck of avoidance
will come to an end.

Is there a way I can
impress on you the way I feel?
Have I no appeal?

If it doesn't work
it's not the end.

'Cos in me you know
you'll always have a friend.

Just let me *know*,
if I should go on hoping, living…

is there an answer *by Scott E. Force*

for you

Where does it all go
from here, up, I assume
as there is a prominent
change, noticeable and alienating
to the once near, possibly forfeited
dear friends.

'o lust for spring and
Renewal, this cold and infertile winter has
Stricken down from the sky
Sun and the majestic ELM.

mr. fix it

Tape it up,
the ripped paper letter.
Glue it back,
the broken flowerpot.
Put a concrete patch
on that broken heart of yours.

is there an answer by *Scott E. Force*

on the side

There on the side,
It can't be HIM.
He looks familiar,
Only from another time.

I knew him once,
He was a very peculiar guy.
He was always looking for the answer,
He only wanted to fly.

It's almost as if
I knew it all along,
The way he hinted at it,
He know the world is wrong.

It can be so hard to
find the way out.

is there an answer by Scott E. Force

ignore

Leave it alone,
maybe then it will
work out.

Leave her alone,
maybe then she will
begin to see it.

You feel til it hurts,
but she seems not to care.
I've seen it before,
it seems to happen everywhere.

as it should be

The way it should be,
as I love her, she *would*
love me…

is there an answer by Scott E. Force

losers

Losers are
Ever being
Taken for painful trips.

Maybe it's fun
For everyone else.

Kindness will
Never be
Openly shared
With them.

did i stutter

J-J-Just let m-m-me know,
W-W-What I sh-sh-should d-d-do.

T-T-Tell me how I c-c-can have y-y-you,
B-B-Because I have t-t-to know.

is there an answer by Scott E. Force

yesterday needs tomorrow

Who needs it?
I ask you this
Question
Completely out of reference.

Who needs it?
I ask you time
and time again.

Who needs you?
The answer is one
You've known all along.

Who needs you?
It is I
and you damn well know it.

Who needs me?
From what I see, there is one thing
of higher supply than demand.

Who needs me?
I wish I know.
I once thought you.

Who needs you?
Yes, I see you finally
did guess, I do.

Who needs it?
I sure don't, 'cos
I'm running out of hope.

Who needs it?
I may not, you may.
If you're gonna call, make it today.

I don't need it.
I need you.
I wish you would need me.

My end will come soon.
You'll look for me tomorrow,
but you'll find me gone yesterday.

is there an answer by Scott E. Force

you know

Who knows
the name
of the man who
went away,
Hoping and
Helping.

Do you know
Who it was?
Who he was?

Yes.
You do,
although you
Refuse to acknowledge it.

And you
Know
Who it was
Who died
that tragic death.

You know who he was.
You know why he was.
Why can't you see
what you're doing?

You killed me,
You knew it all along.
You just let it go on.

Why don't,
didn't, you care for me?
I gave you all,
You took it all.
I'm so stupid,
so sad.

If there was only
some way to
show you what
you've done...
to me...

is there an answer *by Scott E. Force*

teasing

Is there
A reason why
you
seem not to care,
when
I call to you?

It's as if
you
don't want me to
call.

What am I to do.

Just tell me if
there's a reason,
let me know now,
'cos I think you're teasin'
me.

is there an answer by Scott E. Force

the candle is out

Don't let it end this way...
Sure, it sounds like
an overused cliché.
But isn't that what I am?

Let me know how it is you feel,
the danger, in your mind,
it is not real.
That's what you make of me.

Take it or leave me,
I've just no more time to waste.
You've blown out the candle I lit.
Look what I've become.

hold

The hold you have over me is
quite inexplicable in its
infinite power and complexity

is there an answer *by Scott E. Force*

the big world

I'm sure that
at one time
I had a friend.

Someone who would
listen to me.
It's just so damn vague.

I sit here - alone.
I don't feel at home
anywhere I go.
It's all mixed up.

This world is
So big...
I'm lost.

This world is
So small...
I've no room to live.

None at all.

is there an answer by Scott E. Force

how may i help you

The ring of the phone
never comes to my ear.
Is it too much to ask,
for you to show you care?

If I wait any longer,
I know I'll go insane.
I'd be surprised if you know my number,

Even know my name.

Don't I do enough for you,
with my calls to ask,
"How was your day?"
You greet me with an artificial mask.

What is it in me that
I should change
for you
to call out my name?

is there an answer by Scott E. Force

hey?

Hey,
What about me!

Can I come along on this
Fabulous train ride?

Come on, let me, I'd like to see you
as you feel inside.

Hey,
What about me!

Why are you running
away from me?

Is it something I said?

What do you want
me to be,
'cos I'm lost…
almost dead.

is there an answer by Scott E. Force

there you go

So you've come back again,
I'm happy to see you.
What's that you say?
You're just seeing how I am?

Well, I'm fine on my own,
with others, or alone.
But the way you are acting
it seems you'll soon be gone.

Again.

yon

Was there ever a time
when peace flowed throughout the world,
and it was true then,
that Peace of Mind flowed in men?

Carry me back to that time of old.

is there an answer by Scott E. Force

clear

I wish you were glass,
such that I could see inside you,
take a good look at what
you are made of, that
has such a hold overt me.

I wish you were glass,
a pure and clear globe
through which I could
see life clearly,
less severely.

Unfortunately, you are of diamond,
sparkling and colorful,
when held at the correct angle.

You cut me to shreds,
you're so hard I almost dread your
your touch.

is there an answer by Scott E. Force

waiting

Well, here I sit,
alone in AGAIN IN
my room,
thinking of you,
waiting like a fool.

I hoped you would
call tonight,
but you never did.
You never ever did.
Do you think I'm just some kid?

Maybe I'm too young
to understand
the way things are.

Maybe I'm too old,

And I'm reaching out
too far
for a dream t
that's beyond my grasp.

***is there an answer** by Scott E. Force*

a void

I sit here alone
in a seemingly
eternal
void.

It seems I try
so hard
to see you,
but all you
ever seem to do is
avoid.

Me.

what i'd give

I'll give you anything
to impress how much you mean.

I'll give you my money,
I'll give you my car,
I'll give you my Waters
signed bass guitar.

Anything to show
what you mean.

is there an answer by Scott E. Force

imbalance

Worldly possessions
are of no importance
in comparison to you.

I doubt that there's anything
at all,
I wouldn't do for you.

There's always a feeling,
of me giving you
so much
more than you return.

But the problem lies
in the interest you earn.

For you.

is there an answer by Scott E. Force

the end

I see you, but we do not
speak, one to another,
and I wonder why,
'cos I'm sure there must
be the answer
somewhere up there
in the stars,
beyond where I can see.

There must be a place
Where I can force my way,
and haver my way, and
have you, as I've wanted for so
long, far too long,
as my journey is lonely
without you,
and the
end of the line draws near.

So for once, I ask,
lend me your ear as I have
a secret for you.
Ys you, I'm sure you knew it all
along, how enamored I am
of you.

But don't throw the party yet,
for I bring unto you
unfavorable tidings,

As it is I, NOT you,
Yea, it was always
what I made of you that
kept me coming back for
mor., and more, and...
Enough already,
'cos it's starting to show.

Your love of
my attention,
but as is this page
I've come to the end.

is there an answer *by Scott E. Force*

i've got them

I've got them,
those feelings we all know.

I try to escape them,
but they're everywhere I go.

It's just what I don't need,
they dig into my brain.

They cause my heart to bleed;
it's a real emotional drain.

The Green Jell-o Blues.

is there an answer by Scott E. Force

serious

It's a comedy
this game we play.

Why don't you leave,
just stay away.

Let it ends now.

It's a comedy
the way we act together.
You say it's alright,
but I think there's another.

Let's end it now.

It's a comedy
the way we talk.
I think I'll go now,
take a long walk.

Let's end it now.

It's a comedy
this life we lead.
It's you I hate.
It's you I need.

Let's end it now.

is there an answer by Scott E. Force

in the music

```
I think of you,
     Every night,
     Every day.

I'll always love you
     If I might,
     If I may.

Wish we'd see
     There's a light,
     There's a way.

I can hear it in the music.
```

dial tone

```
Here I am,
     All alone,
          And I wait
               By the phone
                    For you to call.
               What have I
          To say?
     Not a single
Thing at all
```

is there an answer by Scott E. Force

a long day

I read the paper, boy.
They say your father's dead –
Don't let it go to your head

There's a lot more to be said
A gun to your head
Look to the bed

Where lies the man
Don't lend him a hand
Now, it's too late

I think it's time we ate
Why do you feel sad?
There's more fun to be had

Feeling left out?
What's it all about
You ask, as any fool would

You'd know if you could
But the answer is far
So go jump in your car

Ram into a tree
What fun it'll be
Hurts bad, don't it?

is there an answer *by Scott E. Force*

This had to come and ruin it
All the fun times there were
How were you ever lured

From the ease of the day
No more time to play
The act is finished

The play was a winner
Time to go home
Now that it's done

Wish there was somehow a way?
A secret escape?
Sorry my friend

I've looked for it long
And I've come to the end of my rope.

is there an answer by Scott E. Force

in the lies

There is a feeling that lies…
    Within my heart,
It tells me, not when to quit,
    Just when to start
I only wish I could understand why.

There is sometimes a sense
    Of deep regretting
I once knew the answer
    But I just keep forgetting.
I only wish I could remember why.

There used to be a closeness that
    We once shared.
I was hurt,
    You were spared.
I only wish I could have realized why.

There is a feeling that lies…
    Within my heart,
It tells me, not when to quit,
    Just when to start
I only wish I could understand why.

is there an answer by Scott E. Force

the new game

It's not easy, coming back...
To the old game...
Nothing much has changed.
Yet it isn't quite the same.

in the dark

How can I be sure
Of who I am anymore,
When I am still in the dark
When it comes to who I want to be.

it's not about winning

Where am I now, you leave me, though I was warned it came as a surprise. How can YOU win??? Who am I to say, as the answer is not mine to know or give - you beat me...

is there an answer by Scott E. Force

not much

I want to be
I want to have
I ask not for much.
Just your love.

Why can't I have you?
Are you too good?
Am I too low?
You're spilling my blood.

in your hat

I view you for
a second, if that.

There you stand,
me in your hat.

Why do I love you
Someone must know
the reason that
I care for you so.

('cos I sure don't)

is there an answer by Scott E. Force

traveled road

The earth below my feet
Heavily trodden o'er the years
When love comes; then he.
Then goes; then she.

Giving way to bare foot and shoe,
The grass, a reflection of days,
Nights past, past.

He knows, she knows.
The pain – manageable,
destructive hell, nonetheless.

WILL IT EVER END?!

is there an answer by Scott E. Force

is there an answer

Why is it
that when I call
you on the phone
you never sound alone
while I sit, in the dark, at home?

I talk to you
but it seems as if
what I say
just does not bite.
I don't want to fight
just to get along
with you.
Just to get along
with my life.

I wish there
was a way for
you to see how
this whole ordeal
is affecting me.
It's killing me.
There must be a way.

Is there an answer?
I ask the questions many
times over

is there an answer by Scott E. Force

and over again
please not again
Let it be
for the first time.

We can start anew.
There is no boundary set
what we can do
me and you
together like we should?
Be...
Who knows.

Ever was there a single
perfect one for me
it would be thee
so far as I know.

But what do I know?!
I thought you cared.

Is there an answer?

is there an answer by Scott E. Force

summer's gone

On a summer day
    You can go to the beach,
    Or have a picnic,
Suck on a peach.

On a summer day
    You can go for a walk,
    Sit by the pool,
Draw on the road with chalk.

On a summer day
    You can go for a jog
    Maybe go camping,
Chop up a log.

On a summer day
    There are many things
    That you can do.
Too bad it's fall.

www.ingramcontent.com/pod-product-compliance
Lightning Source LLC
Chambersburg PA
CBHW061348040426
42444CB00011B/3148